# THE LEADERSHIP JOURNEY

## HOW TO MASTER THE FOUR CRITICAL AREAS OF BEING A GREAT LEADER

**Gary Burnison**, CEO of Korn Ferry
Afterword by **Ken Blanchard**

# WILEY

Cover design: Ross/Madrid

Published by John Wiley & Sons, Inc., Hoboken, New Jersey.
Published simultaneously in Canada.

For general information on our other products and services or for technical support, please contact our Customer Care Department within the United States at (800) 762-2974, outside the United States at (317) 572-3993 or fax (317) 572-4002.

Wiley also publishes its books in a variety of electronic formats. Some content that appears in print may not be available in electronic books. For more information about Wiley products, visit our web site at www.wiley.com.

*Library of Congress Cataloging-in-Publication Data:*
Names: Burnison, Gary, 1961- author.
Title: Leadership the journey : how to master the four critical areas of
   being a great leader / Gary Burnison.
Description: Hoboken, New Jersey : John Wiley & Sons, Inc., [2016] | Includes
   index. | Description based on print version record and CIP data provided
   by publisher; resource not viewed.
Identifiers: LCCN 2015043765 (print) | LCCN 2015047697 (ebook) | ISBN 9781119234852 (cloth)
   ISBN 9781119234869 (pdf) | ISBN 9781119234876 (epub) |
Subjects: LCSH: Leadership.
Classification: LCC HD57.7 (print) | LCC HD57.7 .B86653 2016 (ebook) | DDC
   658.4/092--dc23
LC record available at http://lccn.loc.gov/2015047697

Printed in the United States of America
10  9  8  7  6  5  4  3

TO MY ESTEEMED COLLEAGUES

# INTRODUCTION

# A LEADER'S PATH

Imagine you are standing in Battery Park, on the southernmost tip of Manhattan. The city bustles around you, and on this clear morning you have stunning views of New York Harbor and the Statue of Liberty. History is beneath your feet: one of the oldest settlements in North America. From these early hubs, the western migration of settlers began. Soon, you will follow in their footsteps.

As you stand in the park, you are oblivious to the sounds of the city—the horns and sirens, the pulse of the metropolis. Gathered around you are 4,000 people from 40 countries. And your job is to lead this diverse group of people on a cross-country trip *by foot over the next five years*—from New York to Santa Monica on the Pacific shore, a distance of 2,500 miles by the most direct route. That is the vision, the destination of this organization.

On that early morning, you know that a solitary walker, putting in about 10 hours a day, could make it from New York to Los Angeles in about 90 days. However, you have been given five years (a typical tenure of a CEO) to reach Santa Monica, which means your team of 4,000 people will walk about an hour every day for the next half decade. As you ponder the enormity of leading 4,000 others on such a trek—physically moving them from here to there—you wonder how you will keep everyone motivated and aligned, leaving the familiar for the unknown, losing some people and gaining others, for five years. Sound obscure? Well, not so much.

This is the essence of leadership, of being a CEO: emotionally and sometimes literally transporting people on a journey from one place to another, and inspiring them to believe in what they can achieve—that they can, indeed, reach a faraway destination.

In the flurry of leadership books, from the theoretical to the inspirational, it's easy to overlook the profoundly simple: *The first word in leadership is, literally, lead.* But in order to lead others, you must, first, lead yourself. The change you wish to see in others begins with the person you see in the mirror; it is virtually impossible to improve an organization unless you improve yourself.

People always ask me, "Are leaders born or made?" I have found that it's a little of the former and a lot of the latter. So much has been written about the left-brain side of leadership—the frameworks, theories, decision-making models; these are non-negotiable. What separates great from good, however, is found in the right hemisphere: a leader's ability to inspire others to the point they wake up at 4:30 AM without an alarm clock, excited to keep moving forward.

Effective leaders do the left-brain technical stuff that identifies opportunities and challenges—finding "the opening in the sky." But they don't stop there. They are equally capable of using their right brain to empower others to believe they will make it through that opening in the clouds. Importantly, these multidimensional leaders are also humble, acutely self-aware, insatiably curious, always authentic, and quite courageous.

"Are leaders born or made?"

Adventurous leaders know the topography—the map of the leadership world and the human brain. They understand that throughout the day—from dawn to dark, and often well into the night—they must continuously address four crucial aspects of leadership:

## LOOK IN THE MIRROR

Develop the self-awareness to lead yourself first, with full knowledge of your strengths and weaknesses. Just as your day starts in the mirror with washing and grooming, so, too, your daily leadership begins by looking candidly at yourself, making sure that you radiate purposeful passion—with enthusiasm and authenticity.

## EMBODY PURPOSE

Start with the "why" of any leadership journey, and also define the "how" and the "what." Purpose is the fixed point—the True North—by which to navigate at all times. As the "why," purpose creates alignment to enact the vision (the "what") through the strategy (the "how").

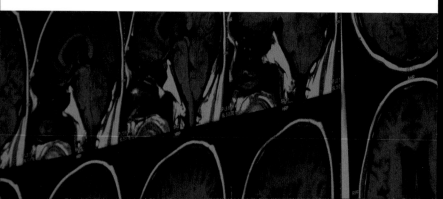

## DON'T WALK ALONE

Remind yourself that leadership is always a journey with others. In fact, it's all about others and what they achieve, which must be celebrated . . . always. Because there is no leadership without followership, you become the message and commit to being "in the moment" at every step.

## NAVIGATE BEYOND THE HORIZON

Plot the course beyond the line of sight of what everyone sees. Refuse to be "the pilot of the inevitable" who drifts on the currents of what is going on around him or her. You anticipate what is around the next bend, but not yet visible, while correcting your course in real time when the unexpected inevitably arises.

To master these four critical areas, the leader looks "outside-in" at the forces that will influence the journey, as well as "inside-out" at the organizational capability and alignment. To lead, you must walk this way—all in, all the time!

Whether you are starting out on your leadership path or you are a seasoned traveler, I hope this little book will be your companion. May it inspire you to discover the adventure for yourself.

— *Gary Burnison*

**Adventurous leaders know the topography—the map of the leadership world and the human brain.**

# Lead · er · ship (n.)

The capacity to lead.

# CHAPTER ONE

EAST TO THE SUNRISE
LOOK IN THE MIRROR

Each day, leaders must be willing to look into a mirror of self-awareness.

**T**he journey is never about the leader, but it starts with the leader. Along the way, the leader is the motivator, navigator, and guide: charting the course, setting the pace, and changing direction when necessary. As a shepherd, the leader keeps others aligned, sometimes by walking in front, sometimes behind, and sometimes beside. The leader's focus is always on others.

By taking a good look in the mirror at the start of each morning, you reflect, assess, and recommit to continual improvement, always asking yourself, "What can I do to make—and be—the change I want to see in the world?"

Undertaking the leadership journey requires self-awareness on the part of the leader. It bears repeating: It's not about you, but it begins with you—who you are as a person and the behaviors and attitudes that you model for others.

# LEADING OTHERS BEGINS
# BY FIRST LEADING YOURSELF

## MEASURE YOURSELF BEFORE
## YOU MEASURE OTHERS.

### TAKE A HUMBLE LOOK IN THE MIRROR.

To lead others, you must continually measure yourself—not overestimating your strengths, and not underestimating your weaknesses. To do so, you must be able to look humbly in the mirror. After all, self-awareness and honesty go hand in hand. Let others illuminate your blind spots as you improve yourself and, by extension, the organization.

### THE ACCOUNTABILITY YOU WANT
### TO SEE IN OTHERS STARTS WITH YOU.

I once engaged my senior team in a live assessment of my leadership strengths and blind spots. I gathered them from all over the world in a hotel conference room to rate me using remote control "clickers" to ensure anonymity. After each question, the results were immediately displayed at the front of the room. It was intense, to say the least. As insightful and appreciated as the feedback was, that wasn't the real purpose of this exercise; it was to demonstrate a willingness to be vulnerable.

As the leader, I wanted to model for my team the vulnerability of being willing to look in the mirror—in this case, publicly and transparently. That's why, at the end of the three-hour session, I gave each person a small mirror as a reminder that a leader can only inspire and motivate others if he or she is willing to undertake an honest self-assessment. Only by looking in the mirror can they ask themselves such things

*As the leader, you are responsible for what goes on in your organization.*

as whether they were truly willing to be vulnerable around soliciting and accepting feedback.

As the leader, you are responsible for what goes on in your organization. Model the leadership behavior that empowers others. The changes and accountability that you want to see at every level start with you. Your attitude and actions cascade throughout the organization, creating followership. So believe it, say it, mean it, and act it. Consistency is paramount.

## SURVIVAL OF THE SELF-AWARE.

Leading others on a long journey (literal or metaphoric) demands many capabilities, traits, experiences, and skills. You must be smart and have the required expertise—all the things that got you to a leadership position in the first place. In addition, you must possess an array of other skills and attributes—the motivation to lead, the interpersonal skills to connect and communicate with others, the ability to inspire other people, and so forth. Without this palate of competencies, your leadership journey will probably be a very short jaunt.

What's the secret ingredient for leadership success over the long term? Self-awareness. As Korn Ferry has found in its extensive research and work with senior executives, self-awareness is a crucial, make-or-break trait. Why? Without self-awareness you will not see your blind spots—and virtually all leaders (nearly 80 percent by our assessments) have them. Blind spots amount to overestimates of skills. You think you're this, but you're really that. You think you are very good at inspiring and motivating people, but they don't feel it. You think you're exceptional at strategy, but others don't perceive you that way.

Having a mirror to reflect who you are is great. But you need to be able to see it clearly. Self-awareness clears the fog.

## YOU ARE THE FACE OF THE ORGANIZATION.

As an operating officer, you can be "one of the guys." Even though you've been promoted several levels from where you started out, other than having increased responsibilities, the shift in how you are perceived probably doesn't change all that much as you climb the pyramid toward the top of the organization. Then you approach the pinnacle. Once you step over that threshold from the number-two level to number one, everything changes.

Standing at the top, the apex of the pyramid, you experience a colossal difference. As "the" leader you are viewed as a function first—the CEO—and a person second. It's not about you (it never is, don't forget). It's about the job that you represent.

I learned the "you are a function" lesson as a newly promoted CEO when I attended a formal dinner in South America. It started late, as is the custom. It seemed to go on and on until we were three hours into the event. It was well after 11 o'clock, and I was jetlagged and exhausted from traveling. Yet no one had left yet. I didn't want to appear rude to the hosts, so I waited for others to get up. No one did. Finally, as it approached midnight, I mentioned this to someone sitting next to me. "Nobody has gotten up to leave as yet because you haven't," he explained. It was my first taste of the truth that, as the CEO, when people looked at me they didn't see "Gary," they saw "the CEO"—the role that I occupied.

## FIND A CONFIDANT/CONFIDANTE FOR YOUR "GRAY DAYS."

When people view you through the lens of the leadership function, you no longer have the same freedom you once had. You are the face of the organization. Because of that, the people around you will begin reading your mood like tea leaves. If you seem worried or preoccupied, then people will wonder if they should be worrying, too! On those "gray days" you can't radiate your doubts, worries, and concerns. However, you do need confidants/confidantes to help and advise you, ideally someone who has walked the same path: a CEO for a CEO, a coach for a coach, and so forth. With these trusted advisers who understand what it means to occupy a leadership position, you will have help and guidance as you fulfill your obligation to be "on" 24/7.

## THE JOB IS NOT YOURS FOREVER.

Here is the paradox: As the leader, you must fully and totally embody that function as a steward of the organization, the role model of the purpose and vision, and a shepherd of the team. As all-encompassing as that job is, though, it doesn't belong to you.

In the time-collapsed world in which we live, tenures are often relatively short; the same is true for coaches of major teams and senior leaders of other organizations. In any leadership appointment, you don't have a lot of time—and the job can be taken away from you. Being a leader is not a lifetime appointment.

Recognize that the end point of your leadership is not the end point of the organization. You are part of a leadership continuum. Your job is to be a source of energy and change to grow the organization, and to be a steward during the time of your leadership. Being a leader is more about who you are than what you do.

"My job is to recruit, attract, and compensate people; provide a moral compass; match their skill sets to different needs in the organization that I'm running, whether it's a company or a government; and then to make sure that they work collaboratively and collectively."

—Michael Bloomberg, former Mayor of New York, and Founder, Bloomberg L.P.

# RADIATE PURPOSEFUL PASSION

AS THE LEADER, YOUR JOB
IS TO INSPIRE PEOPLE SO THEY
CAN EMPOWER THEMSELVES.

## LET THEM SEE YOUR
## PASSION FOR THE PURPOSE.

People will not always agree with the leader. But the
one thing that should never be in question is the leader's
passion for the organization and its purpose. More than anything, the leader's passion must be seen and felt throughout
the organization.

People rarely follow someone because of their plan of
action—what we're going to do next. What excites people
is passion for a purpose—a gravitational force that will pull
them in to the shared vision. It comes back to the "why"—
knowing the purpose and believing in it so much that you
embody it.

## TAP THE POWER OF STORYTELLING:
## EMOTIONALIZE YOUR MESSAGE.

Whenever I interview people, I never ask what's on their
resume. I'm looking for something else—the way the person
thinks, how he or she engages with others, how he or she
creatively solves problems. Recently, I asked a candidate,
"How many quarters would you have to stack to reach the top
of this building?" The answer was immaterial. I just wanted to
know how the person would handle such a question, whether
puzzling it out or making a wild guess. What the person did,
though, was question the question. He just couldn't figure out
why such a thing was relevant (of course it wasn't—but that
wasn't the point). In the end, the person wasn't hired.

Engagement and interaction say more about you than any list of accomplishments in a bio or on a resume. I remember being told by a hiring manager many years ago, "I know what's on your resume. Tell me about you. Tell me a story so I can really know who you are."

Storytelling and personal engagement extend far beyond the job-seeking process. As the leader, you are the master of your organization's narrative. Just as the shamans of old gathered people around the fire at night to share the tribal wisdom and lore, so, too, the leader is the keeper of the organizational story. People will feel the force of your passion and commitment in the stories you tell and the actions those stories reflect. They will believe—and they will become inspired to act. When you emotionalize your message, you will move others to consider what they, too, might become if they were "more"—more determined, more prepared, more confident, and more empowered.

## WHEN DID YOU FIRST FEEL EMPOWERED? USE THAT FEELING!

I can still remember the first time I rode a two-wheel bicycle: my dad removing the training wheels from my shiny Schwinn, his hand firmly on my back as he gave me one hopeful and final push, and then I pedaled down the pavement as if I owned the road.

We never forget these first moments when we felt freedom, joy, and accomplishment in what we mastered. As the leader, your job is to inspire them, evoking in others that same feeling of riding a bike for the first time, so that they become empowered. Remember, you cannot empower people; people must do that for themselves.

*To be inspirational you must:*
1. Be yourself;
2. Demonstrate authentic belief in the organization's purpose;
3. Make an emotional connection with your audience—your customers and your employees.

## AUTHENTICITY TRUMPS CHARISMA ANY DAY, IN EVERY WAY.

Late-night infomercials with the charismatic salesman describing how you, too, can make millions if you just buy the instructional CD. The magnetic pitchman at the county fair inspiring you to purchase kitchen knives that never dull, all for an incredibly low price that you have to finance over five years. Or, perhaps on a more positive note, persuasive politicians such as Franklin Roosevelt, Bill Clinton, or Tony Blair.

Looking at your own skills, you may wonder, "How can I put in what Mother Nature may have left out? Can I be that inspirational?"

To be "inspirational," you don't have to be Churchill-like. Rather you must: 1. Be yourself; 2. Demonstrate authentic belief in the organization's purpose; and 3. Make an emotional connection with your audience—your customers and your employees. This is the essence of leading others: knowing yourself first and leading others.

When you are an authentic leader, people will trust what you say and mirror what you do. Then purpose, passion, and commitment will scale and cascade throughout the entire organization.

## RAISE PEOPLE'S SIGHTS TO SEE WHAT IS POSSIBLE—WHAT THEY CAN BECOME.

Empowerment means enabling and equipping others to make decisions that are directionally aligned with the organization's vision and purpose. People grow as they are stretched. As the leader, you are accountable for making sure they are not stretched too thin. Your ability to empower others is all about raising people's sights and instilling belief and confidence in what they can do.

*Your ability to empower others is all about raising people's sights and instilling belief and confidence in what they can do.*

"Empowerment as leadership is not me giving something to you. It's helping you find the resources so that you can empower yourself."

—Peter Guber, Chairman and CEO, *Mandalay Entertainment, and Filmmaker*

# CHAPTER TWO

# TRUE NORTH
# EMBODY PURPOSE

The leader's journey is from "what we've been" to "what we will be."

bright point in the night sky—the star, Polaris, the astronomical "True North"—has guided explorers, adventurers, and travelers from time immemorial. Even today, before charting any course, travelers must orient first to their own True North to find their bearings.

Your leadership journey, too, starts with the True North of Embodying Purpose, the "why" of the journey. With a clear and compelling purpose, you set the strategy and gather the people who will join you on the journey. Here you will ponder the basic questions: Why are you making the trip, how will you travel, and who will go with you? As a leader of others (in our example, thousands of others), you cannot expect people to follow blindly. You will need to show them the True North of Embodying Purpose so they, too, can embrace the "why" of the journey.

For the 4,000 people walking from New York to Los Angeles, there could be any number of "whys"—to build a team, to challenge themselves, to support a cause, to make a difference.

Just like the few who have scaled Mount Everest, these intrepid long-distance walkers may be motivated by the desire to accomplish what only a few have ever done. Where there is purpose, there is hope of succeeding—and exceeding what anyone thought possible.

On every leadership journey, the specific "why" will be unique to each organization and its desired destination. What is universal to all is the importance that everyone understands that specific "why." The more people embrace the purpose, the more likely they will follow—not only at the beginning when adrenaline is pumping and excitement is running high, like at the start of a marathon, but later on when the going gets tough, and people question whether they can go another step.

As their guide and co-voyager, you must reflect on what matters most. With this knowledge, you will be better able as the leader to align the group to the overarching purpose and passion, so that they can carry out the strategy all the way to the final destination.

# START WITH THE "WHY"— THE PURPOSE OF THE JOURNEY

## DEFINING THE "WHY" ESTABLISHES THE VISION AND CREATES ALIGNMENT.

### PURPOSE PRECEDES THE FIRST STEP.

Leaders and followers alike must understand the "why"—the purpose of the journey—before they can take the first step along a path that will take them many years and thousands of miles (literally or figuratively).

Over the years, I've seen leaders jump ahead to the "how" and forget the "why"—in other words, the organization's purpose. Obviously, every leader must set the destination or the vision (the "what") as well as the strategy (the "how"). Similarly, every organization must make money, and every team must win; these are table stakes. The real question, however, is always: "Why?" Why is the organization in business? Knowing that "why" drives and sustains employees' motivation.

### WHY THE "WHY" IS SO IMPORTANT.

Most people want to grow, learn, win, and be part of something bigger than themselves. They yearn to contribute to the journey, knowing that what they do and who they are matters. In short, they want to be loved.

On the leader's journey toward the envisioned destination, everyone wants to see themselves as an integral part—that's why the "why" is so important! When the leader is clear about the "why," real transformation happens, because now everyone can not only see the vision, but picture themselves as part of it. They know what it means to "win" and feel supported in achieving that goal for themselves and the team. Therefore, to foster alignment across an organization, the leader must

define and communicate the "why"—the purpose—to every member of the team.

## KNOWING THE "WHY" CREATES THE SHIFT FROM "ME" TO "WE."

The reality is that thousands of employees could be making hundreds of decisions every day. You will not be looking over their shoulders, nor could you. Rather, your job is to paint the left and right lines, set the destination, alter course if needed, and, most importantly, anchor the organization in purpose. Giving people a sense of "why" they are doing what they do transforms self-interest to shared interest.

When your employees have a strong sense of purpose, they are more likely to act in concert with the mission and objectives of the organization. People will row in the same direction, to the same finish line. As a leader, your responsibility is to cast purpose as the long shadow over the organization.

## PURPOSE IS THE KEY TO CULTURE FIT.

Over the past several years, our firm has completed several acquisitions—all strategic in terms of expanding our reputation as the leading global people and organizational advisory firm. What makes an acquisition successful, though, is not the numbers on paper, no matter how good they may look. It's all about the culture—in particular, blending the cultures of two

organizations into one. The best way to do that is with alignment around a common purpose, bringing people together to pursue the greater "why." Without that alignment, culture clashes will likely happen, which can derail even the most strategic-looking merger.

When our firm makes an acquisition, I personally make numerous phone calls to as many as 100 people in the acquired firm to talk about our purpose—our "why"—which is all about changing people's lives. (I also have continuous conversations within the firm around the strategic advantage of a particular acquisition, which is always discussed in terms of our purpose.) These open, candid communications help keep our culture grounded in the greater purpose, which is essential at all times and even more so during an acquisition.

When one company acquires another, the result may be a "Noah's Ark": two of everything, and sometimes in key positions. Aware of the overlap and redundancy, people become nervous. Ambiguity about what will happen to their jobs can quickly lead to mistrust and trigger the departure of key people. The same people who made the acquired firm attractive in the first place could very well be the first ones heading to the exit! However, when people understand and embrace purpose, they can see themselves more comfortably as part of a new, expanded team. The more they grasp and embody the overarching purpose, the more they will ultimately drive the long-term success of the acquisition. That's why the acquisition is not an end point, but a beginning—starting with alignment around the "why."

## THE COMPANION OF PURPOSE IS VISION.

If purpose is the "why," then vision is the "what." Vision is best thought of as the picture of "what" is to be accomplished—"what" the organization will look like when the purpose is realized. Together, purpose and vision form the basis of leadership. Although leadership styles may differ, purpose is always the driving force behind achieving the vision.

## DESCRIBE THE VISION WITH WORDS THAT RESONATE.

What is your vision? Can you describe it in a way that others can see it clearly? If it's vague in your mind, it will be impossible for others to see it. That's why companies set their destinations with "vision statements" that vividly paint purpose.

In 1980, Steve Jobs's mission statement for Apple was, "To make a contribution to the world by making tools for the mind that advance humankind." LinkedIn evokes community-building in its mission: "Connect the world's professionals to make them more productive and successful." Outdoor clothing and gear company Patagonia offers an all-encompassing statement that succinctly describes a vision of doing good in the world: "Build the best product, cause no unnecessary harm, use business to inspire and implement solutions to the environment crisis." IKEA's vision is as straightforward and functional as its line of home goods and furnishings: "…to create a better everyday life for many people."

What makes a mission and vision statement meaningful is not the eloquence of the words, but their sincerity and authenticity, as embodied by the leader and modeled for every person on the team.

As we discussed purpose, Ken Blanchard, author of the Afterword, recounted this story from his days of teaching at the University of San Diego School of Business Administration, where he always gave out copies of the final exam on the first day of class so that students would know exactly what they were expected to learn. The rest of the course was devoted to helping students master the concepts and material. Ken's university colleagues, however, were up in arms. Why would he do such a thing as giving students the final exam from the beginning of the class? Ken explained his purpose—his "mission statement" of what he intended the outcome to be: "I don't want them to fail," Ken said. "I want them to learn."

## LEADERS RAISE THE "ALTITUDE" OF THE ORGANIZATION.

As a leader, you must embody purpose. It is no less than the basis of everything you do. People need to look in your eyes and sense the unalterable truth of that purpose—what it stands for and where it will take them. The "why" of the journey becomes omnipresent—on the walls and in the halls.

When people embrace a greater purpose in all that they do, it creates change and inspires possibility. It is the organizational beacon illuminating the horizon—the long-term vision. Purpose is the constant through the agony of failure and the euphoria of success. To understand "why" is to claim an enduring purpose.

# "Every aspect of what we do is driven by the sense of purpose."

—*Indra Nooyi, Chairman and CEO, PepsiCo*

# STRATEGY—
# DEFINING THE "HOW"

## STRATEGY IS NOT JUST
## DIRECTION; IT'S VELOCITY.

### SET THE STARTING POINT.

If the "why" is the purpose and the "what" is the vision, then strategy is the "how."

Strategy is one of *those* words—used everywhere, to the point of losing its punch. Senior executives are praised for being "real strategic thinkers" or "very strategic." Of course they should be; that's a given! However, strategy is more than just the road to travel. It also encompasses how you are going to travel, when you will launch, where you are going, and the time needed to reach the destination.

### REMEMBER THE "CATERPILLAR EFFECT."

Strategy begins with an assessment of today's reality, not tomorrow's promise. Most people are familiar with the "butterfly effect," which states that seemingly small or even insignificant causes (a butterfly flapping its wings) can have enormous impacts (stirring the wind until there is a tornado). I like to think of strategy in terms of the "caterpillar effect," which inherently contains the most important elements of strategy: reality and pacing. The "caterpillar effect" reminds us that a caterpillar cannot be a butterfly while it is still a caterpillar. Its transformation is a process, grounded in the reality of today. If the caterpillar ignores that reality and decides it can fly—pushing its capabilities prematurely—it won't get off the ground. You can't rush the process.

Caterpillars take time to turn into butterflies, just like organizations take time to launch, grow, transform, and progress

*"There is nothing in a caterpillar that tells you it's going to be a butterfly."*

—R. Buckminster Fuller

into their next stage of development. As R. Buckminster Fuller said: "There is nothing in a caterpillar that tells you it's going to be a butterfly." But just as surely as the caterpillar will become a butterfly (the transformation "strategy" is embedded in its DNA), an organization with a solid strategy grounded in reality will be able to "take off" into its next iteration. But it starts with *reality* and requires the right *pacing of the process*.

## YOUR STARTING POINT:
## TAKE A "SELFIE" OF TODAY.

The starting point of strategic thinking is a "selfie" of today—both outside-in and inside-out. Outside-in considers influences of external forces, including customers, megatrends, competitors, product innovation, and so forth. Inside-out looks at the internal forces that address the external, such as leadership, people, organizational capability and alignment, infrastructure, technology, and the like. Both perspectives are needed to draw the strategic road map—setting the how, when, and where—once again, starting with today's reality.

## STRATEGIC VELOCITY IS AS IMPORTANT
## AS STRATEGIC DIRECTION.

Here's a leadership truth: You can't move an organization faster than its people and culture can absorb. Even the best strategy on paper isn't any good if you can't execute it on schedule. A brilliant plan that only gets halfway there is a failed plan. The finesse of leadership is shifting the culture and direction of the organization at a pace that matches your organizational capability as well as your strategy. Establish the sequencing and know the gating. Don't stop connecting (and communicating) the dots between why and how—the purpose and strategy.

## PASSIONATE EMPLOYEES AND DELIGHTED
## CUSTOMERS DRIVE SUCCESSFUL STRATEGY.

How do you know your strategy is working? Some organizations use revenue and earnings growth, shareholder value, and so forth. While important, these "hard numbers" are not the determinants of your success. As a leader, it's so easy to get caught up with so many different things that you lose sight of what is ultimately the most important. The catalysts and arbiters of your performance are your employees and customers.

If employees are passionate about the purpose and customers are absolutely delighted by how that purpose relates to them, then your organization's strategy is on the right track. In fact, with passionate employees and delighted customers you almost can't help but hit your outcome targets around revenue, profits, shareholder values, and so forth. But don't mistake the outcomes for what really drives them; it's all about the employees and the customers.

At Korn Ferry, we know that engaged colleagues and enthusiastic clients are the only true means to success. Employees who are motivated will tell others how much they enjoy working at the firm, a place of real purpose and impact—as evidenced by all those satisfied customers!

Satisfied clients will tell other potential customers about our services. After every client engagement we ask: "How did we do?" I feel an indescribable sense of pride when I run into executives around the globe who tell me, "Your firm really changed my life." (I recall an executive who went through an extensive leadership development program and eventually became CEO of his company. When I saw him after his promotion, he was beaming with gratitude to the firm.) We want to know how and where we satisfied them and exceeded expectations, and if there are any areas in which we fell short.

By paying attention to the two factors that matter the most—employees and customers—a virtuous circle is created that leads to continuous improvement.

# DO SWEAT THE SMALL STUFF.

"Don't sweat the small stuff," the well-known adage advises. If you want to have passionate employees and enthusiastic customers, however, it's all about the small stuff. For a retailer, that means knowing what it's like to be a customer who browses the merchandise in the store. Online, it's all about the experience on the website. The same "mystery shopper" approach works in every business, to see your organization through the lens of your customers.

At Korn Ferry we frequently become the "undercover boss" when we do due diligence before making an acquisition—to see if that firm's attitude toward excellence in customer service matches ours. For example, several years ago when we were in the midst of acquiring a company with a well-respected line of leadership products, we called their sales department late on a Friday afternoon. Without telling the salespeople who we were, we ordered several leadership products and explained that they had to be delivered by Monday morning. We were very pleasantly surprised when, on Saturday morning, those products were delivered to a private residence.

Whether you take the undercover approach within your organization or for a company you are thinking of partnering with or acquiring, you will get feedback that can't compare with customer satisfaction surveys alone. Only by putting yourself in the shoes of the customers can you know if the organization really does sweat the small stuff.

"Work that is done well is not only a responsibility to one's self and to society, it is also an emotional need. You cannot live without doing something; [you need] a direction in life."

—*Carlos Slim, Entrepreneur, Investor, and One of the World's Wealthiest People*

CHAPTER THREE

FACING SOUTH

DON'T WALK ALONE

When there is trust in what you say, there will be belief in what you do.

**W**ith self-awareness and knowledge of yourself, you are ready to take on the responsibility of leading others. It is a full-time commitment, taking you from "sun to sun."

Recall the starting point of our story: the southernmost tip of Manhattan, where 4,000 people gathered at the start of a five-year, cross-country trek. Facing south, that leader knows he is not a solitary sojourner.

Neither are you. On your leadership journey, don't walk alone.

Every leader is in the "what" and "how" business—the strategic imperatives of what must be accomplished and how it must be achieved. Ultimately, though, a leader is in the "people business." Despite all of the technological innovations of the past century, a simple truth remains: People make businesses successful.

The people part of leadership is so obvious, yet so often looked at as top-down, rather than bottom-up. Yes, a leader must be a strategic thinker, decision maker, risk taker, and responsibility owner. But there is much more: being a coach, a guide, a teacher, a motivator. Over time, your results will be only as good as the people on your team.

# PEOPLE MAKE THE JOURNEY SUCCESSFUL

TO LEAD IS TO COACH; TO WIN YOU MUST HAVE THE RIGHT PLAYERS ON THE TEAM.

## THE SIMPLE TRUTH: IT'S ALL ABOUT THE PEOPLE.

To be a leader, you can't journey alone. Leadership requires followership. To create followership, leaders must meet people where they are. To lead is to make an emotional connection on a very real and human level in every interaction. As a leader, you must commit to meeting the needs of those who follow. Think shepherd: occasionally in front, sometimes beside, but mostly behind.

The best leaders always focus on the other person. What matters most is not what the leader accomplishes, but what others achieve.

## WHO'S ON THE TEAM?

It comes down to talent. Without the talent, there is no performance. Think like a coach, drafting players who fit the offense for today as well as for tomorrow. In other words, pick people who can evolve with the organization's strategic direction but also fit the reality and culture of today.

The leader can't be the star player, scoring all the points. Rather, the leader is committed to helping others do their best. As the leader, you facilitate from the sidelines, but you are never removed from the front line, ultimately accountable for the results of the team. That's why it's the players who win games, but the coaches who lose them.

. . . OCCASIONALLY IN FRONT,
SOMETIMES BESIDE,
BUT MOSTLY BEHIND.

## CHOOSING PEOPLE FOR THE TEAM: LISTEN FOR THE "WE."

Being in the talent business, we are often asked about how people really get noticed. This perspective also gives us insight for what leaders should be listening for as they bring together a team. Most important: Listen for "we" and not "me." People who aren't afraid to use "we" in their success stories showcase their self-confidence by willingly giving credit to others. This is far more impactful than just saying "I'm a team player" but having no evidence of that fact.

In addition, listen for the way people make emotional connections—the energy with which they speak. Does the person speak with confidence and authority? If so, then you have an indication of how well he or she will connect with coworkers, team members, clients, and others. In addition, the way the person uses stories demonstrates his or her ability to enliven communication and connect with others—expressing ideas in a way that makes other believe.

## TAKING THE FIRST STEP.

Start with the purpose, the vision, and the ensuing strategy. From there, contemplate the skills, competencies, and leadership characteristics needed for each initiative in the plan. Ask yourself: How should we appear in front of customers to achieve our vision? Hire, train, and develop against these attributes.

Having the right ingredients alone is not enough; they need blending. You must smooth rough and jagged edges of individuality into one continuous, unified mosaic. Your team must become a harmony of talents and abilities that complement each other, not simply a team of "yes." Continuously measure alignment of the team to the strategy.

Last but not least, when selecting the team, consider hunger to learn and curiosity as tiebreakers over pedigree any day.

"In show business, the show comes first, because if you have a great show, you will have a great business."

—*Daniel Lamarre, CEO, Cirque du Soleil*

# CELEBRATE ... ALWAYS

LEADERS WHO HOLD OFF ALL CELEBRATION AND RECOGNITION TO THE END OF THE JOURNEY WILL LIKELY FIND THEY ARE TRAVELING ALONE.

## CELEBRATE THE INCREMENTAL ACHIEVEMENTS.

Direction plus time are the primal elements of measurement that must be part of every journey of taking people from here to there—as well as from the past to a future of their own design. This is not a journey measured in months and miles, but rather in milestones, celebrating each achievement along the way to turn discouragement into encouragement, the mundane to the miraculous. (As Ken Blanchard observes, the leader is always "trying to catch people doing things right!")

## WIN THEIR HEARTS AND MINDS, NOT THEIR POCKETBOOKS.

The bottom line is that people want to know that they belong, that they matter. They want to contribute to something that is bigger than themselves—something with purpose and meaning, that makes the journey worthwhile, regardless of when (or if) the destination is reached. Leadership fosters belonging—developing an emotional connection. When you say to your team, "Your contribution makes a difference" and "You are important," what you're really saying is "You are loved." Showing your respect and appreciation to the team is transformational.

## WE NEVER REALLY GET OUT OF THE SIXTH GRADE.

Even as adults, we never really move beyond the desires and motivations of the playground. We want to be liked, to be accepted, and to have what everyone else does. We want to be popular, to stand out, to win—otherwise, we're taking our toys and leaving the sandbox! Self-interest rules.

Self-interest is intrinsic in everything we do, from the companies we build and operate for profit, to the charitable acts that make us feel good about ourselves. This is not to denigrate such activities, but rather to shed light on what drives human behavior—the need to survive and the desire to thrive, which we all share. It becomes the leader's job to meld individual self-interests into a kinetic, moving force for good, to advance the overarching goals of the organization, community, or even society as a whole. Then self-interest *(I want to know I make a contribution, I want to feel that I matter, I want to be loved and appreciated)* is elevated to the point of morphing into selflessness, and a common commitment to the greater purpose of the journey.

## MOTIVATE BY NOTICING, COMMENTING, AND ENCOURAGING.

It sounds so simple, even obvious, but it's not. For the leader, this part of rewarding and celebrating can be elusive. Leaders who manage by walking around are often exceptional motivators of people—simply by noticing, commenting, and encouraging. I have found that the simplest things can be exponential motivators: sending a gift to a team member's spouse or partner, even a parent; an e-mail or handwritten note; a call to say a simple "thank you." These have the subtle but powerfully motivating effect of tossing a pebble in a pond—the words ripple throughout the organization. Use purposeful praise with employees; celebrate progress by praising extraordinary efforts, not just final results.

## REWARD DOES NOT ONLY MEAN "MONEY."

Yes, money is important—certainly in the top five, but it's not number one in employee engagement. Money is simply a satisfier, not a durable motivator. I have found that if people only join your organization for money, you are just "renting" and they will ultimately leave for money. The true rewards are reaped by transforming self-interest to common purpose.

More important than "the money," however, is whether it is equitable within an organization. With compensation, focus first on the "why" (the behavior you want to elicit) and much later on the "how much." As a leader, you have to continuously measure and ensure the alignment of the compensation and incentive process to the strategy and behavior you are trying to drive (as in that age-old saying "show me how they are paid and I will tell you how they will behave").

## IT'S THE SMALLER THINGS THAT MEAN THE MOST.

As the leader, you are involved in compensation of your team: salary, bonus, and benefits. The entire package may also include such things as flexible work arrangements (e.g., telecommuting) and tuition reimbursement. As we have found, while people are grateful for their compensation, salary, bonuses, and perquisites, these elements are not what generate the biggest reactions and the most complimentary feedback. The most significant outpouring is generated by the smaller (in terms of monetary value), more heartfelt gestures.

At Korn Ferry, we've seen this with an employee recognition program called our "Founders Awards," which are given out every quarter to recipients who are first nominated by their peers and then selected from a pool of candidates by a committee of peers across the firm. One recipient was so overcome with emotion after receiving the award he was literally in tears of gratitude.

The same thing happens at holiday time. Our employees are in 40 countries around the globe, with diverse cultures and backgrounds. For the past couple of years, in recognition of our success and wanting to say a special thank–you to every employee, we've sent out 4,000 gift cards in a nominal amount, along with a note from me that I take quite a bit of time composing.

People want to be compensated fairly, and deservedly so. But touching their hearts is often done through small gestures that truly make them feel seen.

> "We believed in owner-ship. . . . So people did well if our shareholders did well. We had a real community of interests."
>
> —*Eli Broad, Venture Philanthropist, The Broad Foundation; Cofounder, Kaufman & Broad (KB Home); and Founder, SunAmerica*

# YOU ARE THE MESSAGE

COMMUNICATION BUILDS ALIGNMENT
AND EXECUTES STRATEGY.

## IT'S NOT ONLY WHAT YOU SAY,
## IT'S HOW YOU SAY IT.

A leader is never not communicating. When I first became CEO, I was oblivious to a pervasive reality of leadership: I was so focused on the "message moments" and their content—bold speeches, judiciously worded e-mails—that I failed to notice that I was still broadcasting the rest of the time, and with the rest of my body. Everything I said and did not say, the words I chose or avoided, the relative ease of my gait, where my eyes focused, whether I used this story or that one, told it in a voice calm or commanding . . . a message imbued each of these seemingly tiny or insignificant details. The skill with which I mastered each mattered—a lot. Remember, as a leader, it's not simply about staying on message—you are the message!

## LOSE THE POWERPOINT SLIDES.

Communication is where leadership lives and breathes. Don't underestimate the impact of the nonverbal.

As Peter Guber, the Academy Award–winning producer and businessman, once told me, "When a leader walks into the room, before he or she speaks the first word, people already have formed an opinion. . . . Language is an art to express ideas, but energy is what is projected." Make an emotional connection with your audience—use stories, not bullet points.

**REMEMBER, AS A LEADER, IT'S NOT SIMPLY ABOUT STAYING ON MESSAGE— YOU ARE THE MESSAGE!**

## PAVE A TRUE "INFORMATION HIGHWAY" THAT FLOWS IN TWO DIRECTIONS.

Every voyage requires a feedback loop of two-way communication, listening to what people say (and observing how they say it), and learning all the way. There must be communication to build alignment and execute strategy. Eighty percent of communication is listening—and making it safe for others to tell the truth. Learning is what keeps you on the track and able to outpace the rest.

Keeping on track, over rough and often uncertain terrain, requires agility—that is, *learning agility*. A key predictor of success, learning agility allows leaders to manage the new and different, by applying lessons learned to unfamiliar and first-time experiences. Leaders who are agile learners absorb information from their experience and use it to navigate unfamiliar terrain.

## INHALE BEFORE YOU EXHALE; THINK BEFORE YOU SPEAK.

Your road is the "high road"—always, with no exceptions. As a leader, there's no room for offhand, ill-considered remarks. You are not speaking for yourself, you are representing others. Therefore, always use "we," "us," and "our" versus "I," "me," and "my."

People will also take you literally, so be clear and precise. Just as your words can be inspiring, they can be enormously de-motivating. Become more conscious by zooming out before you speak; always ask yourself if the words will result in the desired outcome as they are cascaded throughout the organization.

## GUIDE OTHERS IN WHAT TO THINK ABOUT.

As a leader, you must use communication to move beyond telling people what they need to know, and instead guide them to what to think about. In order to do this, you must first understand your audience—what they are thinking. From this place of knowledge and compassion, you move beyond merely speaking the words—to become the message.

The higher up the organizational ladder people go—from individual contributor to manager to leader—they become less action oriented and task oriented, and much more reflective as creative thinkers. I remember a conversation I had with a surgeon (I was seeing him for a minor procedure) during which we talked about our respective occupations. Hearing that I was a CEO, the surgeon shook his head and said, "I wouldn't want that job—too much responsibility for all those people!" I was shocked! A surgeon literally has someone's life in his or her hands. However, while the skills of a surgeon obviously require a high level of expertise, this profession is still largely task oriented. A CEO must be primarily a self-aware, creative thinker capable of leading others through highly complex challenges and scenarios—telling them what to think so they can act accordingly. Rise above. Leadership is grace, dignity, and restraint.

"Never did I think of giving up, because of all the employees I was responsible for . . . Once I establish a goal, I will never give up until it is reached."

—Liu Chuanzhi, Founder, Lenovo Group Inc.

# BE IN THE MOMENT

LISTENING, A LEADERSHIP SKILL, INVOLVES
OBSERVING WITH EYES AND EARS—
DETECTING THE TEXTURE AND CONTEXT
THAT HAPPENS BETWEEN THE WORDS.

## LISTEN TO OBSERVE, ABSORB, AND CONNECT.

The distance between hearing and listening is thinking and understanding. Listening is observing, absorbing, and connecting. The message you must broadcast in that moment is that no one is more important than the person speaking to you. This is old school. You can't listen and do anything else. No gadgets or computer screens. Listening means looking into the other person's eyes and seeing what words alone do not convey. Also, don't just listen—show you've listened. Words motivate, but actions inspire.

## LISTEN TO EDUCATE YOUR INTUITION.

Communication is 80 percent listening and inquiring, and 20 percent speaking. The former must guide the latter. The problem is that humans, being emotional creatures, love to talk and talk. As soon as someone takes a breath, they are ready to jump right in to fill those awkward pauses. Don't! You will learn so much from what's not said in addition to what's said.

## MAKE IT SAFE FOR
## OTHERS TO TELL THE TRUTH.

There is no freedom of speech unless one has economic independence (and very few of us have that). In other words, people will generally defer to the most senior person in the room. Being in front of the leader naturally makes people hesitant or guarded. They filter what they say, with a bias toward the "good news" or what they think the leader wants to hear. As the leader and the most senior person in the room, you have to make it safe for others to speak. Listen to what you don't want to hear, listen without judgment, and never, ever, seek retribution for something somebody said.

*Listen to what you don't want to hear, listen without judgment.*

"The talking part of my job is probably the smallest part. I listen to people. When I have conversations with people—talking and listening—it gives me insights that I can't get by reading."

—Ali Velshi, former Chief Business Correspondent, CNN

# CHAPTER FOUR

# HEADING WEST
# NAVIGATE BEYOND
# THE HORIZON

Leaders see what others cannot. They paint a picture that others cannot yet envision.

**T**he mapmakers of old drew the known world—the continents and coastlines, oceans and oases, borders and boundaries. They knew their homelands of Europe, and the trade routes that had taken Marco Polo and others into Asia. To the west, though, lay the unknown—uncharted, unexplored, and inhabited by monsters. Those intrepid explorers looked west to anticipate what lay beyond the horizon, in preparation for one day sailing out of sight of the known world. These true voyagers were undeterred by those blank spaces scrawled with pictures of sea monsters and leviathans.

Journeys today require the same skills, as the leader anticipates what is likely to appear around the next bend or beyond the horizon, which others cannot yet see. In the metaphor of walking from New York to California, the direction is clear and the route is mapped out, but there will still be uncertainties, from weather conditions to detours for opportunities that arise. Changes along the way will be constant!

The leader starts with the reality of the "here and now" and uses intuition and intellect to project the next leg of the journey, based on what is anticipated. No matter how clear or concise the vision, however, conditions, terrain, and climate can change dramatically—and must be navigated in real time. What was expected to be smooth sailing suddenly becomes a turbulent sea. Or, the winds shift favorably and fill the sails, allowing the organization to sail far ahead of its competitors.

# ANTICIPATE WHAT IS AROUND THE NEXT BEND

MEASUREMENT UTILIZES THE MARKERS THAT DELINEATE THE JOURNEY.

## YOU CANNOT NAVIGATE IF YOU ARE NOT IN THE PRESENT MOMENT.

Navigation happens in real time, moment to moment. To be a leader/navigator, you must be (in the words of Ken Blanchard) the "president of the present." Today's reality is the starting point. But if you only look at your feet, you won't get where you need to go. For that reason, as Ken also advises, you must be the "president of the future." Both—at the same time. As the leader you are constantly going back and forth, between the present you see and the future you want to realize, in order to generate the momentum that keeps the organization moving forward. Otherwise, you will only be the "pilot of the inevitable," thinking that you're charting the course while, in reality, you're only riding the currents swirling around you.

## YOU CAN'T LEAD WHAT YOU CAN'T MEASURE.

As compelling as the destination is, for much of the journey it is an elusive, faraway target. The more intangible the end result, the more people will wonder (and grumble): "Are we there yet?" The answer can be provided by measuring, producing data that tell people how far they've come and how much more they have to travel. Measuring utilizes the markers that delineate the journey into achievable segments, which can then be acknowledged and celebrated.

Actively measuring and monitoring means paying attention to the signs and signals. Astonishingly, this "pilot error" is far too common in aircraft and organizations. One of the leading causes of crashes in private planes is running out of fuel. Ignore the gauges and the warnings, and being the "pilot of the inevitable" can result in a tragic end.

## FOCUS ON RELEVANCY.

Earlier in my career, when I was an executive at another company, we sent out so many reports to internal stakeholders, but never received any feedback on them. One day I decided to stop sending reports. More than 30 days went by and nobody noticed. We had been simply overwhelming employees with too much information. This realization prompted us to recalibrate our "dashboard" of measures and metrics—the feedback and data that were most important—and not simply repeat what had always been done.

If the data being collected and analyzed aren't relevant, they waste time and energy that should be focused elsewhere. Only by measuring and monitoring what matters most, can the leader get past the initial launch sequence to the next phase of sustained travel, when the starting point is far behind.

## IT'S NOT JUST THE DATA,
## BUT WHAT YOU DO WITH THE DATA.

As surely as the sun rises in the east and sets in the west, so the vision of the journey needs execution to become reality. And execution needs systematic process and relevant measurement to become effective strategy. That is obvious. All companies do the expected: measuring the top and bottom lines, margins, costs, and so forth. But that's just the beginning. More important than the results and the data gathered are what you do with them.

## SCRUTINIZE WINS AS MUCH AS LOSSES.

Regardless of outcome, immediately after a game, a great coach always watches the tape. Any leader must do the same, particularly when things are going well. However, the data and input you receive will only be as useful as your ability to filter, contextualize, and sound-check. When you measure, you will discover what does not work—the ideas and concepts that looked and sounded promising, but turned out to be disappointments and failures. Even the best of journeys can get off track at times. Trying and failing, however, is not a mistake. The only real mistake is "failing to fail"—which means you aren't innovating.

## LEAD OUTSIDE-IN AND INSIDE-OUT.

Leadership does not happen behind a desk. It's found among the people, both outside-in (checking with customers and other external stakeholders) and inside-out (gathering feedback from employees). Leaders who don't follow this thinking do so at great risk.

Walk around, get around, and be around others who are sharing the journey with you. For this to be effective, however, you must welcome what you may not want to hear—looking for what's wrong in what's right, and what's right in what's wrong.

FOCUS

"The vision of the journey needs execution to become reality."

# ANTICIPATING BEYOND THE KNOWN

ANTICIPATION SETS THE COURSE,
CREATING A MAP FOR OTHERS TO FOLLOW.

## ANTICIPATING MEANS HAVING A PLAN C FOR A PLAN B.

As a leader, you must look around the next turn in the road—
tapping the brakes before the turn, accelerating through the
curve—and always having a Plan C for Plan B. Be urgently
patient. Just as there are four seasons, there will also be cycles
in business. When the weather is good, not only reap the
harvest, but just as important, disrupt complacency. You must
also anticipate "winter," the fallow and changing times ahead.
Those who put away during summer will have the ability to
be more strategic during winter, when opportunities arise.

## ANTICIPATE LIKE A CHESS MASTER— THINK SEVERAL MOVES AHEAD.

A leader expects and predicts, but doesn't guess. As the late
leadership guru Warren Bennis once told me, the future
that is anticipated is based in the reality of today. To create
change, you must meet people where they are, not where you
want them to be. The same is true for anticipating—accurately
perceiving the present, so that you can extrapolate meaning
for tomorrow.

## MAKE ANTICIPATING A TEAM SPORT.

Foster an organizational culture of world-class observers who continually gaze outside-in. Answers are usually in the market, not in the halls. Leaders do not rely solely on their own intuition, but rather encourage and enable diversity of thought to bubble up rather than simply cascade down. They actively seek out the perspectives of others, tapping people's views of today's reality and what that means for tomorrow.

## STRATEGY IS NOT LINEAR.

Make strategic thinking dynamic, not a once-a-year exercise. I've always been amused by the arcane annual off-sites—they are only 11 months too late. Strategic thinking is far less about planning in the calm than it is about decision making and course correcting in the midst of the storm. It is the essence of navigating, making real-time decisions to avoid collisions, overcome obstacles, and capture opportunities. Strategic thinking must be perpetual. At all times, it is better to have a strategy that is 75 percent perfect, but 100 percent executable, than a strategy that is 100 percent perfect, but only 75 percent executable.

"It starts with how you view reality. The leader's job is to get people to look at the present and not just try to read the tea leaves."

—The late Warren Bennis, former Distinguished Professor of Business Administration and Founding Chairman of the Leadership Institute, University of Southern California

# NAVIGATING—COURSE CORRECTIONS IN REAL TIME

NAVIGATING TAKES OBJECTIVITY AND CLARITY—IDENTIFYING OPPORTUNITIES, ADMITTING MISTAKES, AND MAKING REAL-TIME DECISIONS—TO CHART A NEW COURSE FORWARD.

## NAVIGATION REQUIRES AGILITY.

With navigation, you lead in the moment—real-time adjustments and decisive course corrections that are grounded in reality. To navigate means making proactive, purposeful decisions. It requires agility in the moment yet a focus on the horizon—the company's vision and purpose. This is leadership's equivalent to surfing: paddling against a current, choosing the proper wave, and bailing out at the right time.

Navigating with agility also means navigating at 38,000 feet—knowing the entire airspace—as well as when to take the wheel. You are responsible for the totality of the organization. Sweat the small stuff!

## COURSE CORRECTING HAPPENS IN THE MOMENT.

Not so long ago, I was on a flight from Hawaii back to Los Angeles, a trip I've made numerous times with my family. We were already in our seats when the pilot boarded the plane. He wore a short-sleeve shirt, unbuttoned at the neck, and his hair was a little on the longer side. Strapped to his flight bags was a guitar. "What are you going to play?" I asked him. "Dylan," he replied with a smile.

"Oh, I love Dylan," I told him. A moment later I turned to my daughter: "This is going to be an interesting flight." I half

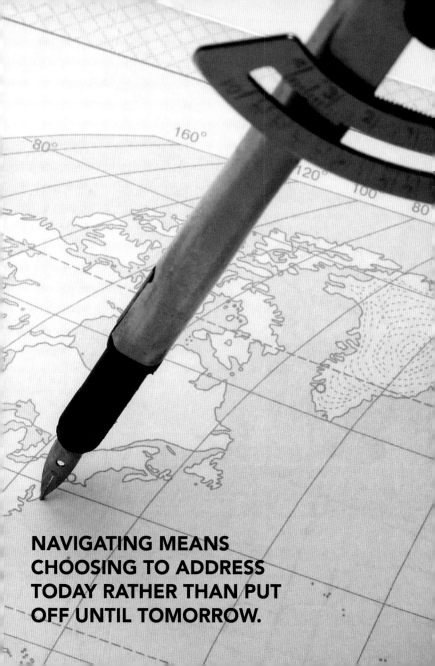

**NAVIGATING MEANS CHOOSING TO ADDRESS TODAY RATHER THAN PUT OFF UNTIL TOMORROW.**

expected our pilot, who looked like he'd be more at home on the beaches of Waikiki than in the cockpit, to start crooning "Hey, Mr. Tambourine Man." Instead, there was a much bigger surprise.

In the middle of this routine flight, with clear skies and no turbulence, our plane made an emergency evasive move—a 600-foot dive in a matter of seconds to avoid a head-on collision. Those gut-churning 60 seconds felt like 60 minutes on a runaway roller coaster, with a sharp drop that put my stomach in my mouth. During the dive some of the passengers screamed. When the plane stabilized, a wave of relief swept through the cabin. The copilot announced on the PA system that another aircraft had been in our airspace. In other words, we almost had a head-on collision.

That laid-back, Dylan-playing pilot navigated in the moment—correcting course almost on instinct—and saved our lives.

None of that could have been anticipated when we took off from Hawaii. However, as part of the extensive training for pilots, such emergencies *are* anticipated. When an urgent situation arises, flight crews know what to do in a split second because the contingencies were identified long before.

Leaders of organizations might not face those same types of life-or-death situations. They will, however, face

mega-turbulence at some time. A perfect example is the financial crisis and the "Great Recession" that followed, which created "navigation challenges" for organizations—whether averting disasters (though some could not be avoided) or finding opportunities.

In the surrounding chaos, our firm oriented toward opportunity, not crisis. This isn't to say that we didn't have to make difficult decisions. We did, but we made these choices immediately and navigated decisively—and all because we had anticipated the problem well in advance. (Although obviously we did not foresee the depth of the crisis or the near-collapse of the banking system, I had said publicly in September 2007, however, that an economic downturn was coming.)

With the view that a downturn was coming, we prepared a contingency plan anchored around opportunity and confidence: preserving the brand and as many jobs as possible, and, equally important, positioning the company for growth as we accelerated out of the economic downturn. When the recession hit, we were ready.

During the crisis, Korn Ferry completed three strategic acquisitions, launched online and offline marketing initiatives, and added employees in strategic markets, which enabled us to significantly expand our talent management business worldwide. The result has been post-recession growth that has substantially outpaced that of the competition. Using the twin skills of anticipating and navigating, we moved the organization from uncertainty to certainty.

## DON'T HAVE "SHINY OBJECT" SYNDROME.

Saying "yes" to everything is not a strategy. Similarly, don't start the fire. Not only do you have to fend off distractions, you must make sure you are not creating any. As a leader, there is no room for offhand suggestions; you will be taken literally. Time, effort, and money can easily be wasted upon your unintended "command." Just as you have to personally elevate the important and delegate the urgent, you have to also make sure this happens organizationally.

There will always be more to do than resources to do it. Ideas are infinite; bandwidth isn't. A good team can identify 20 different initiatives to do; a great team chooses a handful and relentlessly executes, measures, and adjusts.

## TO NAVIGATE IS TO DEAL WITH REALITY.

Immediately confront the unavoidable, the unpleasant. You may be able to avoid reality; what is truly unavoidable, however, will be the consequence of having avoided reality. "Let me think about that" can be as toxic as "that's the way we've always done it." A lack of decision making fosters uncertainty, creating organizational paralysis, which can be deadly. Weigh alternatives, risks, outcomes. Navigating means choosing to address today rather than put off until tomorrow, especially in people-related decisions. Sleeping sentries will end in less than optimal results. Plan a little, think a lot, decide always.

"Visualize a target—and every target has a bull's-eye. Companies will have a far greater likelihood of being successful in achieving their mission if they have a clear sense of what that bull's-eye is, because they can always make sure that's where the first dollar of investment goes."

—*Jeff Weiner, CEO, LinkedIn*

# BE THE CATALYST OF CURIOSITY

EFFECTIVE LEADERS HAVE AND DEMON-
STRATE LEARNING AGILITY—THE ABILITY
TO LEARN FROM PRIOR EXPERIENCES AND
TO APPLY THAT LEARNING TO NEW OR
FIRST-TIME SITUATIONS.

## INCITE ORGANIZATIONAL CURIOSITY.

Create a culture that asks "why not" rather than "why"—
encouraging disrupters of complacency, catalysts of curiosity.
Examples of cultural curiosity can be found in the new technology space, where organizations crackle with energy and
life. Everyone is engaged and passionate about the mission
and the vision.

No matter what your business or industry, you can incite
the same curiosity and willingness to experiment with the
new and different. Orient the organization toward a belief that
the only failure is failing to fail.

## WHAT YOU LEARN TODAY DETERMINES YOUR SUCCESS TOMORROW.

What you knew yesterday got you to where you are today.
However, today is only the starting point for tomorrow.
While you always keep your gaze on the horizon, you have
to start with the reality of today. To lead is to be a world-class
observer.

The distance between your company and its competition
is not absolute; it's relative. You must grow your organization
through learning, outpacing the rest. Remember that although
achievements fade, progress inspires and learning endures.

## BE A MASTER OBSERVER.

Knowledge is what you already know. Wisdom is acknowledging what you don't know. You don't need to be the smartest person in the room, just the most aware. Study the past; observe what's happening in the world; find new and different things to do, places to see; dabble in things that seem entirely unrelated to your business, providing metaphors that innovate your thinking—so that you will know what to do when you don't know what to do.

"History can give you a tremendous amount of perspective. I've learned from history that so much of leadership is helping people deal with change and understand how change happens."

—*Drew Gilpin Faust, Historian, President, Harvard University*

DESTINATION

# LEADERSHIP

**N**ow, five years have passed. You and your team stand on the beach of Santa Monica, California. You made it! Your success came from the most important components of the leadership journey:

**Look in the mirror**—developing the self-awareness to lead yourself first with full knowledge of your strengths and weaknesses.

**Embody purpose**—the "why." At every juncture purpose is your fixed point—your True North—by which you navigated.

**Don't walk alone**—always remembering that leadership is a journey with others. Because there is no leadership without followership, you become the message and commit to being "in the moment" at every step.

**Navigate beyond the horizon**—plotting the course beyond the line of sight of what everyone else can see. You anticipate what is around the next bend but not yet visible, and correct your course in real time.

These are the constants of every leadership journey, no matter where the organization is headed. To be effective, leaders must have deep capabilities in the "solutions business," charting a course around and through the obstacles ahead to reach the desired goals. They must learn from failure, thrive on competition, work hard, and radiate hope. Leaders are flexible, adaptable, and open to feedback, while believing strongly in the journey and its purpose. As their world changes, effective leaders continue to learn, bend, and flex, as they develop and demonstrate their learning agility.

Above all, leaders understand that to lead is to define a common purpose that transcends individual self-interest to an organization's shared interest.

On that beach in Santa Monica, the waves rumble to the shores. Magnificent views abound, from the towering cliffs along the Pacific Coast Highway to Catalina Island in the distance. As satisfying as it is to reach your end goal, it is a fleeting moment. A journey, however, is an accumulation of many moments—each a renewal of your aspiration toward the destination. And that's why, as they say, "It's all about the journey."

"... to lead is to define a common purpose that transcends individual self-interest to an organization's shared interest."

AFTERWORD

# THE LEADER'S JOURNEY OF INFLUENCE

**KEN BLANCHARD**

Coauthor of *The One Minute Manager*
and *Leading at a Higher Level*

**W**hen I was six or seven years old, my father took me to my first Major League Baseball game— the New York Giants versus the St. Louis Cardinals. It wasn't just about seeing the game. My father, who retired as an admiral in the U.S. Navy, wanted me to see two players in particular on the Cardinals—No. 9, Enos Slaughter, and No. 6, Stan Musial. "They'll teach you something about values," my father told me.

When Slaughter came up to bat, he hit a ground ball and ran to first base like his life depended on it. That was the first leadership value: "If anything is worth doing, you've got to give it your all. Be like Enos Slaughter running to first," my father told me.

When Musial came up to bat, he was the perfect gentleman. Even when the umpire made a bad call on a pitch, Musial never said anything. That was the second value: Accept what comes your way graciously, and understand that sometimes others make mistakes.

Through those two players I received an early education in leadership values—courtesy of my father, who was one of the most important role models of my life. (Among the others are my wife, Margie, and Dr. Norman Vincent Peale, whom I had the honor of meeting in 1986 when I was 47 and he was 87.)

That long ago baseball game also taught me another important lesson about leadership: Anyone can be a leader, regardless of title or position. Recently, I spoke at a fund-raiser attended by some pretty accomplished people. Yet when I asked them, "How many of you think you're a leader?" not many hands went up. The reason? Quite a few of them were retired and no longer had the big job titles they once held. They equated leadership with a position, instead of seeing it as an influence process. That's why, at The Ken Blanchard Companies, we define leadership as "the capacity to influence others by unleashing their power and potential to impact the greater good."*

Every day, in every moment, each of us has two basic choices: to be self-serving—to think that it is all about us and satisfying our own needs and desires—or to be serving. To serve is to put others first and yourself last. Many great leaders have modeled this mindset and behavior. Those who choose serving—to be a servant leader who focuses on others—will have a far more interesting and rewarding journey.

When Gary Burnison asked me if I would like to write the Afterword to this book, I agreed because he and I share so

---

* Ken Blanchard (and the founding associates and consulting partners of The Ken Blanchard Companies), *Leading at a Higher Level: Blanchard on Leadership and Creating High Performing Organizations*, Pearson, 2010.

many leadership concepts and values. I'd like to give some of my thoughts about the leadership journey described in the four segments of *The Leadership Journey: How to Master the Four Critical Areas of Being a Great Leader.*

Before I do that, let me share a philosophy I have. I think leadership is a transformational journey that includes self leadership, one-on-one leadership, team leadership, and organizational leadership.

Self leadership comes first. That's why I was excited that Gary started off his journey with Look in the Mirror—because effective leadership starts from the inside. Before you can hope to lead anyone else, you have to know yourself and what you need to be successful. Self leadership gives you perspective. Only when leaders have had experience in leading themselves are they ready to lead others, whether one-on-one or in a team relationship. The key to one-on-one leadership is being able to develop a trusting relationship with others. If you don't know who you are—or what your strengths and weaknesses are—and you are unwilling to be vulnerable, you will never develop a trusting relationship. Without trust, it is impossible for an organization to function effectively. Trust between you and the people you lead is essential for working together.

As leaders develop a trusting relationship with people in the one-on-one leadership arena, they become trustworthy. This is great preparation for team development and building a community. Effective leaders working at the team level realize that to be good stewards of the energy and efforts of those committed to working with them, they must honor the power of diversity and acknowledge the power of teamwork. This makes the leadership challenge more complicated, yet the results can be especially gratifying. That's why I was excited by what Gary talked about in Don't Walk Alone.

Organizational leadership is the final stage in the transformational journey. Whether a leader can function well as an organizational leader—someone supervising more than one team—

depends on the perspective, trust, and community attained during the first three stages of the leader's transformational journey. The key to developing an effective organization is creating an environment that values both relationships and results.

One of the primary mistakes leaders make today is that when they are called to lead, they spend most of their time and energy trying to improve things at the organizational level before ensuring they have adequately addressed their own credibility at the self, one-on-one, or team leadership levels.

As you take time at each of the leadership stops along your transformational journey, Embodying the Purpose will play a major role, as will Navigating Beyond the Horizon. These are key emphases at the organizational level.

Now let's take a look at the four segments of Gary's *The Leadership Journey* in the context of my philosophy about the leader's transformational journey.

## LOOK IN THE MIRROR—THE TRUTH RECEIVER

In leadership circles, a lot is made about the importance of leaders being surrounded by people who are willing to be "truth tellers." These people give honest feedback, without sugar coating, about things like the organization's direction, its latest strategy, or the leader's ability to motivate and guide others. While this is certainly important, it is missing one essential element: The leader must be a "truth receiver."

As Gary observes in this book, leaders must begin the day by taking a good look in the mirror. They must see themselves—their strengths and their weaknesses—clearly and with unblinking honesty. To look in the mirror, leaders cannot be ruled by their egos—which I define as "Everything Good Outside"—nor can they think constantly about their own performance and the opinions of others. If they do, their self-worth is up for grabs every day, because no one's performance is great all the time, and people are fickle.

Looking in the mirror also reminds the leader of the "why" that is being served.

If leaders look in the mirror and think only about their own needs, their leadership journey is in serious danger of becoming hijacked by self-interest. Leaders who look in the mirror and ask themselves, "How can I best serve others today?" will have a rewarding adventure of taking people on a quest that will help them see, accomplish, and become more than they ever thought possible.

For the leader, the journey renews at the start of each day with a little quiet time and simple but profound questions: "What kind of leader do I want to be today—serving or self-serving? What do I want to help others accomplish today?" Then, at the end of the day, the leader reflects on how things unfolded. "Did I live up to being the kind of leader I said I would be in service of others? How can I improve tomorrow?"

## EMBODY PURPOSE—SERVING THE "WHY"

Leadership is a high calling, one that demands the best in us. The key is having what I call a compelling vision. Gary calls it the "why." As he explained to me, "CEOs think they are in the "what," and the "how" business. Ultimately, though, they are in the "why" business. They have to identify the why to get people aligned and moving in the same direction."

I couldn't agree more. Establishing the "why" is the leader's job—putting forth a compelling vision that tells people your purpose (what business you are in), your picture of the future (what the future will look like if things are running as planned), and your values (what will guide your journey). All the leading organizations I have worked with over the years have a clear vision that everyone understands and attempts to live by.

When I wrote *Lead with LUV* with Colleen Barrett, former president of Southwest Airlines, it became clear to me why Southwest is the only airline in the industry that has made money consistently over the last four decades. If you ask anyone at Southwest what business they are in, they will tell you, "We are in the customer service business. We happen to fly airplanes." When it comes to their picture of the future, they are clear: "We want to democratize the airways. Our dream is that every American can be with a friend or a relative at a happy time or a sad time." As for the values that guide their journey, their number-one value is safety, because of the industry they are in. They have three values they want all their people to engage in every single day. The first is a Warrior Spirit. This is not combative. It means if you have a job, do it with all your effort. That's why they can turn a plane around faster than any other airline in the industry.

Their second value is one I have never seen in any other organization—it's a Servant's Heart. They hire for character and train for skill. Obviously, they aren't going to hire pilots who can't fly, but they are also not going to hire pilots who show a lack of character. A while back, a pilot from one of the top airlines in the country was applying for a job at Southwest, because pilots love to work there. On his flight down to Dallas for the interview, he was rude to the crew on the plane. When he got to corporate headquarters, where guests are greeted by two wonderful receptionists, he continued his self-serving behavior with them. As he headed upstairs to the People Department (HR), one of the receptionists called and said, "There's a guy coming up who just came through here. I don't know what he's interviewing for, but he was very rude to us. I got a report from the flight crew on his plane that said his behavior was bad there, too." Not only did he not get the job, he didn't even get the interview. The interviewer told him, "I hope this will be helpful to you in the future," adding that Southwest wasn't interested in hiring pilots who think they are a big deal.

Another value at Southwest is a Fun-LUVing Attitude, which follows founder Herb Kelleher's philosophy that you need to take what you do at work seriously but yourself lightly. That's why they are having fun all the time. They had to deal with the FAA for a while because some passengers reported that flight attendants fooled around too much when doing the in-flight safety presentations. In fact, research showed that when the crew used humor during safety announcements, passengers actually paid more attention than if the presentation had been a typical boring monologue.

When the why of an organization is as engaging as Southwest's vision, people will connect with it to derive their own sense of purpose and satisfaction. People will give their all because they understand that their efforts really do matter.

The best organizations I've worked with understand their "why"—the reason they are in business, which is not about making money. Pleasing Wall Street can't be the only "why." Great organizations share the common understanding that their number-one customer is their people. If they take care of their people—train and empower them—those people will go out of their way to take care of the second most important group of people, their customers. Then their customers will become raving fans and spread their enthusiasm, which will take care of the third group, their stockholders. To me, profit is the applause you get for creating a motivating environment for your people, so they will take good care of your customers. When that happens, the why is clear and performance soars.

## DON'T WALK ALONE—THE GREATER GOOD

I learned a leadership lesson early in my life about the importance of your people. When I was elected president of my seventh-grade class, I came home and proudly told my father, the admiral. He said to me, "Congratulations, Ken. But now that you're president, don't ever use your position. Great leaders are great because people respect and trust them, not because they have power." That was the beginning of my realization that great leaders recognize they are only as good as their people.

Leaders who realize their people are their most important customers tend to be servant leaders. When I mention servant leadership to business audiences, they often think I'm talking about the inmates running the prison, leaders pleasing everybody, or some kind of religious movement. What they don't understand is that there are two parts of servant leadership: vision and direction (doing the right thing) and implementation (doing things right). Vision and direction is the leadership part of servant leadership. The traditional pyramidal hierarchy is effective for this visionary aspect of servant leadership, because people look to the leader for vision and direction. While the leader should involve experienced people in shaping the vision and direction, the ultimate responsibility remains with the leader and cannot be delegated. That's why establishing a dynamic purpose for an organization—or as Gary puts it, the "why"—is such a key role for a leader.

But when you realize that your most important customer is your people, the second part of servant leadership, implementation, takes on real meaning. Unfortunately, it's in the implementation role—living according to the vision and direction—where most leaders get into trouble. The traditional pyramid is kept alive and well, leaving the customers uncared for at the bottom of the hierarchy. All the energy in the organization moves up the hierarchy as people try to please and be responsive to their bosses, leaving the customer-contact people to just quack and say, "It's our policy," "I just work here," or "Do you want to talk to my boss?"

The implementation phase requires turning the pyramid upside-down, so that the customer-contact people are at the top of the organization and can be responsible—able to respond and soar like eagles. Now leaders are at the bottom of the pyramid, where they can serve and be responsive to the needs of their people, helping them to accomplish goals and live according to the vision and direction of the organization.

Implementation done well is the servant part of servant leadership. Because now you Don't Walk Alone; you walk with your people and you serve them in a way that makes a difference. If you do that, you'll help people be high performers. And remember: People who produce good results feel good about themselves.

## NAVIGATE BEYOND THE HORIZON— GRASPING THE SITUATION

Every organization is anchored in the present and the pursuit of current opportunities, while continually envisioning the future. The two skill sets are entirely different, which is why I think organizations ought to have a "president of the present" who is taking care of business today, and a "president of the future" who runs the equivalent of an internal think tank to envision what tomorrow will look like.

In essence, we have that in The Ken Blanchard Companies. When my wife, Margie, was president of our company, I wrote a book with Terry Waghorn entitled *Mission Possible: Becoming a World-Class Organization While There's Still Time*. In the book, Terry and I talked about how a lot of organizations have the same people managing the present and creating the future—which isn't a good strategy. If you send people with present-time responsibilities away to plan the future, they'll kill your future, because they are either overwhelmed with the present or have a vested interest in it. With that, my wife decided to step down as president—she actually said, "I've promoted myself upward"—to head the Office of the Future. She has a small think tank whose full-time job is to look into the future and find out what's happening in the leadership field, technology, and the world at large—anything that could impact our business. The Office of the Future has saved us many times. When people stopped flying after the terrorist attacks of 9/11, a number of our competitors had major problems or went out of business because they were familiar only with face-to-face training. But we already knew about teleconferencing and virtual training, things we learned through the Office of the Future.

A key role of a leader is to constantly Navigate Beyond the Horizon and not miss out on new directions the organization needs to go in to stay viable. Having an Office of the Future helps you course-correct in real time so you can avoid the unexpected developments—giant storms, hidden rocks, and treacherous shoals, to use Gary's analogies—that could get you off course.

While it's great to have an Office of the Future, leaders also need to keep their eyes and ears open to learn—and encourage others to do the same. The most successful leaders are helpable. If leaders establish an environment in which people are willing and able to help, the organization is far more likely to become innovative and creative. Most people are brimming with ideas and observations, especially those who are closest to the customers. As Gary observes, in cutting-edge organizations, anticipating and navigating are a team sport.

## THE JOURNEY OF THE SERVANT LEADER

As you can tell, I'm a big fan of servant leadership. Why is that? Because our research shows that people want to be in an environment where they can gain three things:

First, autonomy. People want to be engaged and make decisions. And the leader needs them to do just that in order to propel forward momentum in supporting the organization's goals and values.

Second, relatedness. People want to be known as human beings. We find this to be particularly true of people in the younger generation, who want to know that they count and that their lives matter.

Third, competence. People want to keep learning and gaining new skills. This supports autonomy and enables people to make better and more productive decisions.

These three things define the journey for the leader and for the followers. People know that they are really important, the group is only as good as everyone together, and the group is committed to every individual becoming as good as they can be—and that includes the leader.

To be the leader, you walk with others. You give guidance when they need it, and accentuate the positive with praise every step along the way. Nothing motivates others more than, as I like to say, "catching people doing something right." If people only hear how they did at the end of the journey, they'll lose heart when the going gets tough.

Leading is a succession of day-to-day coaching, reinforcement, and when necessary, redirection. While your focus is on those who journey with you—who are engaged with you in the game—your influence may very well extend beyond that. You just might make a lasting impression on some unknown spectator watching in the stands.

"To be the leader, you walk with others."

# INDEX